The Little Budget Travel Book

The Secrets of a Frequent Traveler Who Goes on Vacation like It's Free

David Ning

The Voice Behind Personal Finance

Website, **MoneyNing.com**

ISBN-13: 978-09841237-0-4

ISBN-10: 0-9841247-0-9

MoneyNing.com

1.0

This book is dedicated to readers of my personal finance site, **MoneyNing.com**. Without your encouragement and support, this would never be possible.

Table of Contents

I. Why The Little Budget Travel Book

The real question should be - Why not? Don't you want to travel more often with the money you saved up? Doesn't it feel good to know that you are spending only half as much while traveling to the same places as others? What if I told you that instead of planning one family trip a year, you can go twice with the same budget?

Every time someone questions the necessity of doing X, Y or Z to cut costs, my response is always "You don't have to. No one will ever force you to spend less money."

If you still want to ask why you need The Little Budget Travel Book, maybe it's time to just close this book and never open it again. You won't miss it, and the cash you could save will never miss you either.

On the other hand, if you are tired of spending a fortune every time you travel and want to learn how you can save some dough and still have an enjoyable experience, read on to find out how I've been able to afford frequent travel without being really, really rich.

II. The Reason Why This Book Exists

Our family was very poor in my early days of childhood. When I grew up, my mom told me that there was a time when she did not eat out or buy anything that was not a necessity for four years straight. My dad was an engineer by training but changed his career to be an operations specialist for an additional $50 USD a month because his old salary was just not enough.

In 1989, we immigrated to Canada. My dad was afraid he could not find a job in the new country, so he stayed behind. From then until I graduated from college, we took a total of one family vacation - a four day trip to Florida.

I now realize that time doesn't turn back and that memories are the only way for us to remember the past. I will never forget the precious few days I spent with my parents at Disney.

Obviously, I don't blame my mom and dad because we didn't have the means to go on vacation back then, but I really wish that my family could have traveled together more often when I was younger.

When I started my blog at MoneyNing.com, I discovered that I could really help people by sharing my tips for frugal living, and one day, it dawned on me: I had to write this book. I had to spread the word on how to travel frugally. I just had to.

III. What The Little Budget Travel Book is

The book is NOT just a bunch of frugal travel tips. It's about how to have more fun, save more money and travel more.

This book is small. I purposely made it small so that you can take it with you. No more excuses for not having enough time to read it. Bring it with you while you travel—it fits in your luggage.

This book is packed with content. It only consists of tips that I know will save you money; it has no fluff. I'm not a proponent of waste, whether it's time, money or anything else.

This book has a notes section at the end. I put it there so that you can write down important ideas as you read along and refer back to them later. How many ideas have you come up with but just forgotten about because you never wrote them down? Don't let it ever happen again.

The book has a mission. I'm not here to tell you frugal travel is effortless, and you won't always agree with what I write. The goal of this book is to help you travel more often while spending less money.

This book must be read and re-read. This is not just a book to kill time. In fact, the more you study it, the more you will remember the words. The more you study it, the more you will reap the benefits.

This book saves you money. The described methods are proven, but it will only work if you spend time practicing them. Don't just read it once and put it on the shelf.

IV. Let's Begin...

Planning a vacation is not for the lazy. It involves hard work, and unless you do it regularly, the process almost always seems to take forever. That's why it's no surprise that so many of us book vacation packages with travel agencies. You pay, hop on and enjoy.

Are travel agencies right for you? Maybe. Are they the most frugal and flexible way to travel? Probably not.

That said, consider this:

If you ever get to the point where the travel planning process gets overwhelming, then go with an agency. It's simple, easy and hassle free. Best of all, the deals (while not the absolute cheapest) are quite good.

If you don't mind a little work and want to save as much money as possible while still getting an amazing trip, you can't miss the rest of the book. Read on.

Before You Even Start Your Journey

Some of the best tips are actually in this section so be sure to stick around for it. Use a pen and a piece of paper (or the notes section at the end of the book) to write down all of the tips that you don't normally do. Write them down (or type them up) and put the collection of tips in a safe place. When you are planning for a trip, use the tips as a checklist to remind you of the savings that you can take advantage of in addition to rereading this book as a refresher.

Why Prepaying Makes Sense

Many people don't like to prepay for travel because of the age-old argument of "giving them an interest-free loan." I, on the other hand, love prepaid packages. Why? Because it's much easier to figure out how much everything is going to cost before you even pack your bag.

Have you ever gone on a trip, brought a bunch of cash and cashier's checks with you and wondered midway through your vacation where all your money went? When you pay for everything as you go, it's extremely difficult to find a good deal on the spot and keep track of your overall spending. That's why the more prepay packages you can find before you even begin your travels, the better! This includes (but not limited to):

Train Fares – You need to spend time planning the routes anyway so it makes sense to buy prepaid packages.

Attractions - Give Mickey Mouse your credit card and book early.

If anything, at least call ahead and ask how much everything is going to cost. This way, you'll less likely be surprised when you run out of money on the third day of your two week vacation!

Finding Hotels that Include Meals

Many small hotels include food and they are usually awesome. Bed and breakfast is one example but basically, the small hotel owners usually include homemade cooking so you get delicious meals that are guaranteed to be authentic. One problem, these places usually don't speak English. That's why you need to understand…

The Power of a Local Friend

In foreign countries, many travel deals aren't advertised in English because most people in the world can't speak (never mind write in) the language. You can pretty much bet that there are deals of all sorts that you will only find out about if you can call or email the owners in the language of the country you are visiting.

Online travel tips from people who are local to a place are usually the best, but those sites aren't always written in English either. How do you find out about them? How about asking your friend who speaks the language to help? Note: One reader loved this idea as well, saying "I like knowing local friends too because sometimes you can stay with them and not have to shell out for a hotel!" Hey, just make sure you let them know how much you appreciate their hospitality.

Back to Travel Agencies

Due to the "buy in bulk" nature of travel agencies, they can sometimes get incredible deals that are worth noting. Even if only part of their plan suits your travel needs, there is no reason why you cannot use just a portion of their packages and pay the full price of the deal if it ends up saving you money.

Old Technology May Still Rule

There's no telling when this trick will stop working, but a phone call to vendors (car rental companies, hotels, airlines, attractions) may still yield the best deal. The online deals are getting harder and harder to beat, but you may still get lucky if you work the phones. Being nice with the sales people on the other line still works best, so be sure to call when you are in a good mood.

Be a Little Flexible with Travel Days

Prices are always based on supply and demand, so sometimes it's much cheaper to leave the day before (or after) instead. Take a look at the dates of your travel plans and see if spending an extra day is worth it. This makes a huge difference around major holidays, so look early and be the first to get your vacation requests approved.

In general though, hotel prices for Friday and Saturday nights will usually have the highest rates with the least chances of deals. Also, try to depart on a Tuesday or Wednesday and return on a Saturday for the best deals on airfares.

Book a Bundle

There are many package deals that save you money if you book hotels and flights together. Basically, the more business you can give them, the better discounts they can give you. You might not get the exact hotel or airline you are used to, but hey, does it really matter that much when you're saving money?

Go Off-Season

Consider taking a trip in off-peak times (going skiing in the springtime, for example, or going to Hawaii in the winter). It's cheaper and, more importantly, less crowded.

When you travel during the offseason, you will find that everyone (waiters/waitresses in particular) is friendlier and more patient. You really will have a better time.

Travel Close to Home

Overseas travel might be your dream vacation, but there are actually many places nearby that are great as well. Remember, a city that is local to you is overseas to someone else around the world.

Off the Beaten Path

Be adventurous and check out those lesser-known places. There's even a chance that you will find a gem that will take you back again and again, as the non-tourist spots are always cheaper. If you are stuck for ideas, here are a few:

Hiking trails – Many cities have great bike and hiking trails for you to explore. If you are close to a river or lake, try boat activities like renting a canoe!

Farmers Markets – Many cities have spectacular famers markets that you can go to on a weekend morning. What you find there might be so interesting that you will go back every week!

Try Booking at Different Times

With today's sophisticated technologies, online booking sites can change rates based on the time and day of the week you book! What I find is that prices usually repeat themselves on a cycle, so try different combinations and see if you can get a better deal once you have figured out the pattern.

Bid Your Own Price

Priceline.com has a great system where you can name your own price on flights, hotels and car rentals. You can't game the system by bidding a zillion times in increments of a penny, but I've always saved money through this service.

More specifically, I regularly get hotel deals that are half the price of comparable advertised rates just by working the bids. Be patient and persistent and you shall be rewarded.

The downside is that you have to prepay for what you bid for when your offer is accepted, but that's something I can live with if it means saving more than $50 a night.

The Beauty of Detail Travel

One of the best ways to drastically cut transportation costs is to actually travel to one place at a time. No city or even country hopping. Just go to one city and stay there for a few days (or even weeks). You will not only see the city in a different light, but you may also get to know its lifestyle better, which is what true traveling is all about!

Deal Newsletters

Travel Zoo (travelzoo.com) does a great job at finding travel deals, and they have a weekly newsletter that lists 20 of the top travel deals found online! Sign up on their website and you may not even need to search for deals anymore.

National Parks

Compared to a stay at a resort or major theme park, a vacation to a national park is much more cost effective, and it can be just as fun! Each park is unique and incredible to visit no matter what time of year it is. With 58 in the U.S. alone, you won't be bored anytime soon since more than 100 different counties around the world have lands classified as National Parks!

> **Bonus!** Go to MoneyNing.com/Budget-Travel-Book/, type in NATIONAL PARKS to get a raw list of all the National Parks in the world.

Reward Points

Even if you aren't a frequent traveler, sign up for reward programs since you might qualify for something eventually. 99.9% of reward programs are free anyway, so there is really no risk in signing up.

Make sure you study the reward program terms and conditions because you can often use the same membership account across several different companies. For example, United Airline's frequent flyer numbers can be used for any airline that is under the Star Alliance umbrella. Try to use as few reward programs as possible, or else you will only have a few points on many programs and not qualify for anything.

Also, those reward programs are getting sneaky because they will expire if there's no activity on the account. Be on top of these programs and know how you can keep your accounts alive.

Take a Spontaneous Vacation When a Deal Comes Up

Most people take their vacation according to certain schedules, but not all vacations need to be planned. When there is a deal, why not just go? For example, I once saw an airline deal for $14 (yes, that's no joke or typo) so with another hotel deal found online, I went to San Francisco for a weekend – all for $80. It wasn't planned at all but:

- The trip was just as fun, and made more interesting because it was spontaneous.
- It delayed my urge to go somewhere else for a while.
- I could cross off San Francisco as a place I never visited.

Hey, I know it's not possible all the time but when you get to chance, it's so worth it!

Don't Give Up Looking for Deals

Even if you have your plans set, keep trying to look for deals. Reservations can often be canceled with a full refund, so if you find a last-minute deal that fits into your plans, take advantage of it.

I went to Las Vegas recently and saved half my hotel cost since a last minute-deal happened to fit my itinerary. Woohoo!

Airfares

I find it amazing that every company in the airline industry is basically losing money. It is unclear how the industry will change as it continues to strive for profitability, but one thing we know for sure is that we will continue to see service cuts and price hikes no matter what these companies say and how much a barrel of oil costs.

While we can't really control how courteous the flight attendants are, we can at least make sure we don't overpay for the experience.

Airline Tickets

Plan in advance and visit discount websites like Expedia or Priceline.com to see if there are better deals. Some travel sites will tack on a service fee ($5 or so), but there are no charges to check out how much your itinerary will cost. So the timeless advice to comparison shop applies.

Note that even with the online price guarantees of the airline's own site, travel discount websites can still save you money. How? They automatically combine flight segments from different airlines because their mission is to provide the cheapest fare, not to keep you with the same airline.

Connecting Flights

You might think connecting sucks, but it sure saves you a good chunk of money if you can afford the extra time. When you opt for connecting flights, make sure you find out whether you need to check-in your luggage a second time at the connecting terminal as that process can take a long time.

Also, know which terminal your plane is landing in and which your next flight is leaving from. In some airports, this means you need to be checked by airport securities again and that some of the merchandise you bought inside the security checkpoint will need to be thrown away.

Let me explain by telling you my story. The U.S. Transportation Security Administration (TSA) does not allow liquid containers to go through the security checkpoint (unless it's less than 3 ounces), so the wine I bought for my father-in-law wasn't allowed through. TSA told me I had two options – either throw it away or step aside and drink it all, neither of which made any sense at the time. I did offer to share it with the officer but that proposal was rejected too. My feelings were hurt, but it was better than being drunk!

Location, Location, Location

You should always check nearby airports to see if there's a great discrepancy with airfares since the extra driving time might be worth your while. This is especially true if you have a connecting flight as it increases the different flight combinations exponentially.

Travel Light

Airlines are starting to charge for everything now, and if you have two bags or more, expect to be charged for it. Remember to not use over-sized bags whenever possible and to try keeping it to one bag per person.

If you are traveling with a friend who travels frequently, he might be able to get extra bags in for free with his airline status. Ask your friend to check the bags in for you, but make sure she knows exactly what's inside as the responsibility lies with the person who checked the bags.

Don't be foolish and pack two small bags when you can get a big one for essentially half the baggage fee. There are rules on the exact dimensions that are allowed, but you should be okay as long as you are buying luggage from a reputable company that designs its bags to the correct dimensions.

Also, you are allowed one personal item as well as a carry-on. Carrying on your purse or laptop bag can help you avoid luggage fees.

Substitute

Consider packing really old clothes for your vacation if you plan to buy new ones on the trip. This way, you can add more clothes without sacrificing luggage space since you will be throwing away your old clothes on your trip.

Of course, make sure you are packing clothing that you are going to throw away anyway. When you get there, don't rush yourself to shop. Replace the old ones as you find ones you like.

It Doesn't Matter Whether It's a Round Trip Ticket or Not

There are times when one-way tickets are so expensive that the round trip ticket is actually cheaper. It doesn't matter how many legs of the trip you are using because you can always get credit for it. Even if you can't, is there a reason why you should buy that more expensive one-way ticket? (I know this seems impossible, but I've seen it and I bet I will find it again one of these days).

Try to Get Back to the Same Airport

Flying in and out of the same airport is almost always cheaper. This not only goes for flight tickets, but for car rentals as well.

For most people, it's not really the origin that changes but the destination. What I mean is, if there is more than one city on your itinerary, schedule your return flight from the same city you flew into. While it may sound great to fly to Orlando, drive to Miami and fly home from Miami International, the extra cost might make it logical for you to take two trips.

Traveling to Two Countries

Many airlines will allow you to stay for a couple of days in the connecting city (or country) for no extra cost. For example, I've visited Japan many times on my way to Hong Kong while traveling with United Airlines because the airline always connects in Narita (a city in Japan) anyway.

This way, you are essentially visiting two countries for the price of one (as far as airfare is concerned).

The easy way to do this is to find out where the major hubs are from each airline because the airlines will almost always fly to an immediately hub and connect you somewhere else. Once you know where the hubs are, see if adding that city into your trip will make sense.

Car Rentals

For most road trips, it's probably better to drive your own car if price is a concern at all. After seeing some of the bills my coworkers file in their expense reports, it might even make sense in some cases to **buy** an old car just for road trips (yes, car rentals can be that expensive)!

Many people like to rent cars because they get to drive something new and they somehow think it's cool, but is it? Isn't cash in your pocket just a little bit cooler? With enough savings, you might be able to buy yourself a new car instead of driving one for a couple days a year.

Be Specific with Car Rentals

One-way car rentals (when the pick-up and drop-off locations are different) are sometimes more than three times the price of standard rentals, especially if the two locations are in different states (or countries).

If you need a car for seven days and will be in one city for five days and another city for two, break the rental period in two and have a five-day same location rental and another two-day one-way rental. You might need to go back to the rental facility, but it really doesn't take that long and it might save you a few hundred dollars.

Usually, only the more expensive companies allow you to do one-way rentals, so breaking them up will even give you a chance to use a cheaper car rental company for one segment of your trip. Of course, you may need at least two people with this method so that you can return the two cars to their respective rental facilities but the little hassle can equal big bucks.

Car Rental Coverage

Some insurance policies and many credit cards have car rental coverage, so take advantage of it when you rent a car. All you have to do is pay with the credit card that will cover you. Just make sure you decline the coverage from the rental company when they ask because, without fail, they will.

Diesel Should be Renamed the Frugal Fuel

Here's a money-saving tip that few people think of: When you rent a car, why not rent one that takes diesel fuel? It can cut your fuel cost almost in half since diesel is much more efficient, so you can literally count the savings while you drive.

I would caution you though that not every gas station (especially in the United States) offers diesel fuel, so make sure you don't run out of gas while driving in the middle of the night.

Airport Surcharges

Different countries give surcharges different names, but they are nothing but costs for travelers like us. A little known trick to pay less for car rentals is to rent from an off-airport location. Not only are the airport taxes all gone, the car rental base price is usually cheaper as well since there is less demand for the vehicles. Most rental facilities close by will even have shuttles that take you to and from the airport, so just ask.

Size of the Car

I always get the smallest car possible because not only do I not need the extra room, I also don't want to pay for the extra gas that bigger cars need. Also, make sure you know what "standard size" means at the company you are renting from as different companies treat these terms differently.

A Handy GPS

A GPS (global navigation system) might be the greatest invention for road trips since sliced bread, but don't overpay the car rental companies for it. At rates of $15 to $20 a day, you can basically buy your own if you rent the car for a week.

Also, companies make you upgrade your car to be able to rent a GPS, so stop feeding those cash hungry companies and keep the money for yourself.

Children's Car Seats

You might think the advice for this is the same as for a GPS, but a child seat is different because it is much bigger. If you are traveling with kids, you might think that bringing the car seat is cheaper, but that's probably not the case. Call the car rental company and ask about rental prices. With airlines charging for extra luggage these days, it might be easier and cheaper to just rent it.

Fill Up that Rental Car

If you are renting a car and need fuel, just fill it up with regular gas (i.e. the cheapest variety) since that's what the car rental company uses anyway. (Note: This is not true if you are renting something like a Ferrari, which is tuned for the high octane that's present in premium fuel. However, if your rental car costs more than $1,000 a day, I need to ask you: Did you spend more than a millisecond contemplating whether this book was worth the money?!?)

Also, decline those services in which the companies fill the gas tank for you. Even though the advertised price per gallon may appear cheap, most people don't know that companies charge you for a full tank of gas regardless of how much gas is left in the tank when you return the car.

Coupon Codes

Sometimes car rental companies have coupon codes that can be used for substantial savings. Finding the codes on the Internet is easy. Just go to Google and perform a search using the name of the rental company and the words "promo code". Read carefully though, as not every coupon code is usable.

V. Once You Arrive

You have finally arrived at your destination, but the opportunity for savings is not over. Chances are good that you aren't as sensitive with prices when you are out enjoying the vacation (don't worry, this is normal), so this section might potentially save you the most money.

I know what you are thinking: "I'm on vacation, but I have to watch every penny and compromise?" Hey, think about it this way. Do you want to go on vacation twice, or would you rather go only once because you needlessly spent all of your money on the first trip?

All of your travel-related choices are personal, but think about the cost of your decisions!

Eating

Most people save money by not eating on vacations, but that's just not the way to go in my opinion. There are too many ways to save and still eat at the same time.

I also believe that an important part of every vacation is experiencing the local food, so not eating is like having only part of a trip. That's not what I would call the "full experience".

The trick is to really know where to go and how much you are going to spend before even getting out the door. Which leads me to...

Planning Your Meals

Figure out your plan for the day and find a restaurant before you actually go out. This is not just good for your wallet, but your stomach too since you will probably find economical restaurants that taste great.

A great way to find out is to ask the front desk of the hotel for recommendations but let them know you want something that tastes great and won't break your budget. Searching online at review sites is also quick and easy. If many people gave good reviews, chances are good that you will like the restaurant too.

Cook for Yourself

Almost no one will do this, but cooking while on vacation can be quite fun. It's different from cooking at home in every way: cookware, dining area, supermarket, etc. If you haven't tried it before, I really recommend giving it a try at least once. You might even fall in love with it! (You can even take a picture of every self-cooked vacation meal and make a photo book to remind you of good memories for years to come.)

Meals that Carry Over

Want a breakfast that costs nothing? Ask for some bread "to go" at the restaurant the night before. To be honest, most leftover restaurant bread tastes better than breakfast that you actually buy at some places anyway.

Remember to have water ready come breakfast time because you don't want to eat bread without something to drink.

Avoid Breakfast from the Hotels

If breakfast at the hotel isn't included, it is probably expensive. It's much better to walk out the front door in the morning and find a local café across the street. Look for places that have a ton of people because they are either good, cheap or both. If you really want to make sure, ask the hotel staff or anyone on the street. You will for sure get a good recommendation, unless you happen to ask the owner of a coffee shop where the best coffee is in town.

Eat More at Lunch than Dinners

Fancy lunches are often much less expensive than dinners while big breakfasts are less expensive than lunches. It's also healthier to eat a big breakfast and a medium lunch followed by a light dinner. This way, you will not only save some money but also have more energy to sightsee.

More is Better on Meals

When it comes to food experiences, variety is sometimes more important than whether you are eating your favorite dish. You might be happier with more, less expensive dishes on the table than with ordering the priciest plate on the menu. Try it and you might be surprised at how satisfying it is when they ask you to move because they couldn't fit all of the dishes on your table!

Transportation

Maybe it's the lack of information on the subject or the lazy brain cell lurking within all of us, but transportation costs are often a forgotten part of the vacation planning process even though they can be a significant chunk of the overall expense. If you plan and buy in bulk whenever possible, you will save big.

Think back to all the trips you've been on in your life. How many times have you really thought about the short commute from A to B? The expenses might seem like small amounts, but you know small expenses add up. Don't be lazy. Spend the extra time on thoughtful planning and cut back on your transportation costs.

Rail, Metro and Subway

Research multi-trip discounts, especially if you are traveling within Europe. Many metros and rails have multi-day unlimited travel passes that might help save you some money. This also gives you more flexibility to jump around different places within the city, as you won't be worrying about the cost of taking many short rides.

With the added freedom, you can walk around town, go have lunch at a totally different place and come back to finish your tour without worrying about extra transportation costs.

Night Trains and Flights

If the ride is going to be long, consider traveling at night to save money on accommodations and much needed time. Many people have a tough time sleeping on these long rides, but I truly believe that it's all in your head. Once you get used to doing it, you will be sleeping like a baby.

The added advantage is that the overnight rides are usually a little cheaper as well since there's less demand. As usual, take the experience that no one else is willing to take for the best bargain.

Take the Slower Transportation

If flying to your destination is too short for you to take advantage of sleeping while you go from point A to point B, take a bus ride! You'll sleep without even noticing that you are traveling, and you can have a really good meal when you get off because the savings are huge.

Avoid Taxis and Welcome Public Transportation

Many tourists travel by taxi because it's seems like the easiest way to get from point A to B, but it's also the laziest. Consider the subway or buses, which are much cheaper and sometimes even easier than a taxi.

By taking the transportation methods that locals take, you actually get to see a side of life that you would never see if you just mindlessly jumped into a cab all the time. The locals might dream about taking a cab, but a tourist like you might find it fun to be in the subway with everyone else.

Driving is Not Bad

Want to just pay the $200 dollars and take that 1-hour flight? With airport security and all of the airport inefficiencies these days, you might as well drive to your destination since it takes just as long as flying. Also, there's no TSA official to recommend drinking a whole bottle of wine on the road.

Once you arrive, having a car is much easier than dragging your bags everywhere, and it also works out great when you need to go buy supplies, groceries and other things.

Walking is Even Better

If your destination isn't that far away, consider asking the locals for walking directions. It's good exercise and it also gives you a chance to see the city and take more pictures.

One time while my wife and I were traveling, we found an amazing ice cream place just because we happened to walk by (oh, it was very good; I want to go back just writing about it). If we took a cab or bus, we would have missed it completely. Sure, we would never know that it existed, but that would still suck.

At the end of the day, we travel because we want to experience the city, and that should include every bit of it. Walk it or lose it!

Currency

The wild fluctuations of the currencies are almost begging for travelers like us to pay attention. Where we used to see small daily moves, we now see fluctuations of 5, 10, even 20% within weeks. Hopefully, this phenomenon won't last long, but in the meantime, beware of the currency exchange rates.

A little tip I got from a friend is to use Google to track the currency rates. You can add the tracking feature to your Google search page so that you will see it every time you use Google (this service is known as iGoogle, where you can add what is known as gadgets onto your own customized Google.com homepage).

Once you add your favorite exchange rates, you will know how your own country's currency is doing against others.

Go with the Weak Currency

If you have not decided on where to go but just want to get away from home, consider traveling to a place where the local currency is weak. Doing this is like getting a discount on everything from food to gifts to hotels--everything! Sometimes the local currency's weakness is so sudden that the reservation systems haven't even caught up to the new adjustments yet. In this case, you might be able to take advantage of short-time amazing deals.

Getting Cash

Many specialized and well-known exchange rate facilities have very bad rates, so don't go there. Since the ways to find the best exchange rates vary by country, search the Internet to find the best value for your money. For example, a simple search indicates that the best exchange rate is found at the airport and by using ATMs in Taiwan and France respectively.

Try Using the Local Version of the Same Website

Due to the rapid changes in currency rates, it can be much cheaper to book your arrangements using local currency. The secret to doing this is to check the local version of the same website you are purchasing from. With some languages, you might need a friend who is a fluent. If you remember picking your country a while ago but can't seem to find the option on the website anymore, your computer (or your browser more specifically) might be remembering your preference. You can either clear the cookies of your computer or find another computer before accessing the page.

Accommodations

Most everyone already spends a good deal of time searching for the best rates on accommodations, so I don't want to give you the usual "comparison shop" advice. These are additional ideas to ensure that you aren't paying for anything extra with your travels.

No hostel or sleep in the train station suggestions either. While it's certainly doable and will save you some money, you will probably worry too much about your belongings getting stolen.

Staying in a Town Next Door

The hotels in smaller, nearby towns are usually much less expensive than those in bigger cities. If you don't mind a 10-15 minute ride each day from where you really want to be, it can provide significant savings.

You can also use the savings and get an upgraded room at a hotel that's not at the heart of the city.

Since you won't know where you are once you are inside the hotel anyway, you'll probably want to be in a nice room rather than a convenient location.

Home Exchanges

These are pretty cool and popular, especially in Europe. Your trip might not be as romantic as the ones in the movies, but this could be exciting and refreshing if you want a different experience.

Once you arrive in your exchange home, you truly get to experience what it's like to live there for a short period of time.

Don't be Afraid to Ask

Sometimes, the receptionist at the hotel front desk can give you free upgrades (or even free nights). If you already have a reservation booked elsewhere, call the hotel and tell them that you would consider changing if you can get an additional night free. This works especially well on smaller hotel chains, but it can work anywhere (a little tip to the receptionist doesn't hurt your chances either).

Vacation Homes

If you are staying at a destination for at least a few days, consider a vacation home instead of multiple nights at a hotel. Vacation homes are bigger and more comfortable, and your cost will probably be lower as well.

Frugal Suites

Instead of having two separate hotel rooms, consider the two-bedroom suites that some hotels provide. A suite will end up being cheaper and you will get just as much privacy.

As an added bonus, suites have a living room for you and your friends (or kids) to hang out.

Pay in Local Currency

Some hotels will offer to convert the charges to the currency of your country (U.S. currency is by far the most popular). Do not be tempted by this because the exchange rates are even higher than what the credit card companies charge. What's more, your credit card company may still charge you a "foreign transaction fee" on top of the exchange rate.

Hotel charges should be an expense that you have factored into your travel plans, so plan to pay with cash to save the most money.

Extra Fees

Most people don't look at the extra fees when they compare prices. That's a mistake because fees can be as much as 20-30% of the base price. Look for resort fees or taxes, which might be different for every hotel.

If you like to stay connected on the Internet while you travel, also check to see if the hotel you want to stay at provides free Internet services. It may sound like a minor detail, but you could be charged as much as $20 for every 24 hours of use.

Also account for the price of breakfast in your hotel stay since not every hotel will provide free breakfast.

A Special Note about Internet Fees on Cruise Ships

Cruise ships are the worst offenders of overcharging Internet usage because the service is unstable and the ships charge as much as 75 cents a minute! If you want to save some money and don't need to be connected 24/7, wait until you get to the scheduled stops and simply ask the captains or the attendants for the closest Internet café.

If you want to do as much as you can online without wasting money while waiting for the sometimes slow connection to load web pages, use the Internet when the ship is relatively stable and at times when others are unlikely to be using it (during meals or late at night).

Shopping

Whether it's the need to buy souvenirs or just the case of the plain old "impulse buying" bug, shopping is part of vacations like day trading is in the stock market. While it's never necessary, there is almost always blood on the streets without it. Just ask my wife. (Did I really just write that in a published book? Ah, never mind.)

Buy buy buy, but be responsible at the same time.

Duty-Free

Many airports have duty-free shops, and most people use them to shop for family and friends whom they are visiting. Duty-free might not be the best deal around on a pre-tax basis, but the tax savings are substantial.

Also, most people don't buy items that they regularly use for themselves (perfume for instance) due to the hassle of carrying them while traveling. This is nonsense for obvious reasons. Buy it if you use it and it's cheaper. It's as simple as that.

Duty-free shops are also a great place to use up some of the foreign currencies that you have left. You will be happy to know that many duty free shops allow you to pay with several different currencies, so take advantage if you frequently go on vacations and have a bag full of coins from every country in the world.

Bargaining is Fun

The smaller the merchant, the higher the chance that bargaining will work. When you are buying anything while on vacation, flex your customer muscles and ask for a discount. Don't worry about feeling embarrassed because everyone does it. Let them know that you are ready and able to buy if you can get a better deal.

Be courteous though, because making friends is always beneficial.

Different Standards

It may be common in the town that you are visiting for merchants to charge "special" (read: higher) prices for tourists. While it may work best if you look "local" and speak the language, it's not always possible for most of the countries that you want to visit. (It's not with current technology, but you never know in the future...)

The key is to observe while you are shopping and see if merchants charge different prices for different people. If they are willing to sell at $10 to someone while they quoted you $20, chances are good that you can just offer $10 (or even a little less).

Another way to get good local prices is to ask someone local to buy it for you. This may be a wild idea for some of you, but it will reap big rewards if you can pull it off. Where do you find these people? Everywhere! If finding someone to take a picture of you never stopped you, why is finding someone to shop with you so hard? This will for sure spice up your trip.

Is it Really Necessary?

Everything always looks cute when you are walking around town. Think back to all your previous vacations and how many useless souvenirs you bought. Can you even find half of them anymore? And the ones you can locate, how many are actually treasured?

If it's not for someone else and it won't add significant value to your memories, you probably can live without it.

Plan Your Purchases

Sometimes, buying goods that are also available at home will offer substantial savings because of taxes and exchange rates. For example, electronics are routinely cheaper in one country versus another based on exchange rates because the price tags are mostly standard. High-end luxury bags are also cheaper in Milan, Italy than they are in other parts of the world. They don't say "Made in Italy" for nothing, you know.

Depending on which country you are traveling from, you may be required to pay taxes on items you acquire aboard. Remember to check your local laws, but luckily, almost every country has tax-free limits on total purchases under certain amounts, so you are okay unless you buy something ultra-luxurious.

Don't Forget About Possible Tax Refunds

Many countries let you get all or part of the retail sales tax back as a refund. Some places make you jump through hoops by asking you to fill out forms, show proof and stand in line, but if you make large purchases aboard, the hassle can save you a bundle.

Always check each country's specific rules (as they might change regularly) by searching online for VAT (Value Added Tax) Refund or Sales Tax Refund online.

Note that with some country's taxes in double digits, this tip alone can help you save substantial amounts of money, so don't ignore it.

VI. The Final Stretch

Make sure you are doing everything you can to save while having fun traveling at the same time.

We are almost there! You didn't think there were so many ways to save money on vacation, huh? If you've been practicing all of these, congratulations! If not, then get off your (insert your own word please) and start saving yourself some dough!

Remember that it's not how many frugal travel tips you know but how many times you practice them that counts. I know it's hard work, but it's worth it because you can enjoy traveling without wiping out your savings every time you pack your bags.

Discount Everything

Some countries have discount stores (I've seen one in Japan, for example) that sell all kinds of tickets at reduced prices. Concerts, trains, theme parks, metro-- you name it, they sell it. Even gift cards for the department store across the street could be on sale, so if you are buying something anyway, taking advantage of discounts will give you instant savings. Just ask around when you arrive at the airport. Who cares if the person looks at you funny? Saving money is serious stuff, and discount stores cans help you cut costs on everything that you will be doing and buying on your trip.

Public Libraries

Remember the local friend who helped you book all your travels? If you are really charming, you may be able to get help finding free passes to museums and public attractions! Some public libraries offer these to residents but as you can imagine, they are always checked out so your friend probably needs to go early and wait in line for them.

Group Discounts

We all know that there are group discounts everywhere. Take advantage by teaming up with a few friends and visiting the same destinations together. You can even arrange it so there is no obligation to be everywhere together.

My coworker used to do this with some success. While it's a little bit of work to arrange everything, everyone ends up being happier in the end because they can travel on a discount and also get the company of others when they want it.

Go to the Grocery Store

Even if you are away from home, it's almost certain that there will be grocery stores at your travel destination. It's worth it to take a trip and get snacks, water, and everything you need for your trip since hotels overcharge for pretty much everything. $3.00 for a bottle of water? No thanks!

Sometimes, I have some fun by leaving a huge empty bag of chips that only cost me $1 by the mini bar in my room that the hotel wants to charge $3 for. You may also want to highlight the fact that it's only $1, which is probably overpriced already!

Age, Student and Membership Discounts

Many attractions like theme parks and museums have discounts for seniors, children or students. If you are traveling, remember to take your ID and membership cards (e.g. AAA card) with you. Just remember to always ask before you pay. Even if you don't get any discounts, it's not like it cost you anything to ask.

Better yet, call those places or look up their websites ahead of time so that you go prepared. Sometimes, it might even make sense to buy a membership card just to take advantage of the savings, as you can probably use the same card elsewhere. Even if you can only use it once, apply anyway if you can save money doing it.

Talk to the Locals

Be friendly and chat with the people that actually live in your destination city. Sometimes, they will tell you where to eat and some may even offer to have you stay over. This works best in small towns where people are usually friendlier than residents in a large city.

Don't believe me? Have you even tried? Didn't think so.

If they let you stay over, they will probably go shopping with you too! (See? It wasn't so hard after all.)

Mini-Tours

I'm not talking about bus tours that take days (these are great too but I just don't like them). I'm actually referring to the one-day tours that take you to many different places within an area. Not only will you get to see areas that you probably want to visit anyway, the bus driver is usually quite entertaining and informative as well.

As a bonus, you may even find some travel companions and build lasting friendships!

Hotels are a great place to find out about tours. In order to get the best deals, you can always call tours up and ask ahead of time, then search online for discount tickets.

Another good place to find tours is, as always, the Internet. You can always find a tourism website for every city and with a list of the tours available for the area. Just search for "[CITY NAME] TOUR" and something good will show up.

Enjoy the Local Version

Many consumables are less expensive when made in the country you are visiting. Consider trying the local food, coffee, or beer (to name a few examples). You might be surprised at how great and cheap it really is.

Another reason to try the local version is because geographical locations produce unique versions of the name thing. Did you know that various types of seafood taste (and look) different just because they live in different bodies of water? If not, I encourage you to experience the difference between lobster from Boston and Australia.

Tourist Spots May Not be That Hot

Many countries have tourist spots that aren't really the most interesting places to go to, not to mention that everything around the area is more expensive. If you've seen it once, there's no point seeing it again and again. Instead, go to local areas and observe life. Not only will it give you a fresh perspective, but people-watching is interesting and also free.

I know someone who loves doing this so much that all she does is fly to a different place and live amongst the locals for a few days every year.

If you decide to people watch, don't stare! Not everyone responds to that pleasantly (don't try, just trust me on this).

Tourist spots not only apply to areas of a city but the whole city as well. Popular places are great, but they are always filled with tourists and everything is just more expensive. Consider lesser-known places for a similar yet more frugal experience.

If you think about it, what's the fun when you see the same types of people in the tourist spots that you see at home? Isn't it more like a vacation when you are trying to communicate with someone who can barely understand your language?

My friend had an interesting experience related to this. He was dining out in a foreign country and couldn't understand the restaurant menu, so he just pointed to a few items when it came time to order. Just as he was about to finish his dinner, the waiter came and tried to explain to him that the restaurant had messed up his order with another table's! Of course, my friend had no idea what the waiter was talking about, so he just kept saying "Okay, okay." The restaurant brought him the dish that he had originally ordered, and he ended up eating a second meal because he felt bad that the food would go to waste! He didn't even know what happened until later when an English-speaking couple came over to explain everything to him.

VII. Bonus

Word on Watching Others

Don't you hate it when those "rich" people line up for first and business class while you are impatiently waiting to get into your coach seat? Actually, it's not as bad as you think. First, the arm rest in business class don't lift up so your children can't recline and rest on your lap comfortably. Second, what's the rush to get into a long and dreadful plane ride? Third, the overseas first class seats are so isolated that you cannot talk to anyone but yourself! Sure, it's nice if you travel alone, but is going somewhere all by yourself what you'd call vacation?

The grass is always greener on the other side! It's never as good as you think.

Tips on Tipping

If you are traveling overseas, some of the best research you can do is to find out about the tipping customs of the country. For example, some countries like Japan will get offended if you tip them, while people in United States expect a tip for services. Below is a guideline of what is appropriate in the U.S. For more details, Wikipedia's page on tips is a great help (http://en.wikipedia.org/wiki/Tip).

Restaurants – 15 to 20%. (Some restaurants may add a standard 18% tip on the tab, especially for large groups.)

Bars – Usually $1 per drink.

Hotels – A couple dollars per bag for the bellmen, and 10 to 15% for room service. $5 - $20 for complicated requests for the concierge, and $3 - $5 a day for housekeeping.

Taxis – 15%, but a taxi driver once yelled at me for giving him less than $2 on a $5 ride, saying that the minimum tip in Las Vegas is $2.

Take Out – 10 to 20%, higher if the weather is bad or you are in an apartment complex with many stairs.

Car Washes – 10 to 20%. More if you want your service person to do a great job next time.

Valets - $2 to $5 when you get the car back, unless there's a standard price.

It's too easy to skim on tips because they're not considered mandatory. However, if the service is good, tips are well deserved! Don't try to save in this area and you will find that the services will improve as people start to treat you even better than good (yes, there's such a thing).

Mini Travel Site Reviews

Many of my readers asked me to include a list of some of the great travel sites out there, so here you have it. The list is based on personal opinion and is meant as a starting point for your research.

Regarding discount sites in particular, I always believe that the more, the merrier because the more you check, the better your chances are of finding a great deal. So remember to check multiple sites whenever you travel, because just one might save you a ton.

Also note that the list is in alphabetical order and there is no preference given to those that are listed first.

Airfare WatchDog (airfarewatchdog.com) – This site is great at catching selective deals that airlines post from time to time. The people behind this site just seem to work harder as they are faster at posting than their competitors and include small airlines like JetBlue as well.

Airport Discount Parking (airportdiscountparking.com) – The website is a little plain, but it offers great discounts and coupons on airport parking, something that so many of us forget to include in our deal searches.

Auto Europe (autoeurope.com) – I have never used this booking service but I recommend it because I have heard that some European car rental companies add hidden fees to your rentals, and Auto Europe will help you dispute them.

BedandBreakfast.com (bedandbreakfast.com) – The site is awesome for finding small hotel deals. If you like the unique experience of lesser-known accommodations (which in my opinion are actually good more often than not), check out this site.

CruiseMates (cruisemates.com) – The site is a great resource (especially for those of us who don't go on cruises that often) as you can find many reviews and information on not only booking a cruise but also things to do once you get on.

CruiseCompete (cruisecompete.com) – This site helps you find agents from all over the world to send you quotes on the exact cruise that you want to take. Since you have to provide an email address (and who knows where that information will be passed on to), I suggest using a separate email account to avoid possible spam.

FareCast (farecast.com) – This site intelligently predicts prices and gives you suggestions on whether you should book right away or wait. The prediction is based on the data collected by the site, so the recommendations are based on science, not marketing (as they claim).

Kayak (kayak.com) – This site has a simple interface that just works. Kayak compares extra fees and different airlines, shows you deals that others are finding and even e-mails you tips on deals as long as you specify which days you are taking your vacation.

HomeExchange.com (homeexchange.com) – With stay durations of usually one to three weeks, this site gives you the chance to come as close to living another person's life as possible. There is an annual membership fee to join, but this is an extremely convenient place to find homeowners who are also interested in home exchanges. Best of all, this site is international, so you could find opportunities to fly overseas to live in someone's house for a three-week stay.

Hotwire (hotwire.com) – What's unique about Hotwire is that it doesn't reveal which company (hotel, flight or car rental company) will give you the best rates. Instead, they just pick the cheapest hotel within the same category for you. For those who are looking for good deals and like trying new companies, this is great because you don't have to worry about which one to pick. To make comparisons better though, they do rank hotels by star ratings.

lastminute.com (lastminute.com) – Forget last-minute, this site has a tab for last-second deals. When I did a test, I found a flight only four hours from departure whose price was comparable to the advance booking price offered by the airline's web site.

LateRooms.com (laterooms.com) – As the name suggests, this site is all about last-minute hotel deals. I don't know how they find them, but they have last-minute deals from all over the world and even let you display the prices in your local currency.

Orbitz (orbitz.com) – Orbitz is one of those travel discount sites that you absolutely need to use for comparing vacation deals. From hotels to flights to cars to cruises, this site has them all. It's interesting that Orbitz charges a booking fee for flights but not car rentals, but don't worry about that because you should compare the total cost.

Priceline.com (priceline.com) – I really love Priceline.com because of their "Name Your Own Price" program. You can really get unbelievable deals using the bidding system. The downsides are that you have to pay up front and you bid on a class of hotels instead of a specific one, but I highly recommend checking this option out.

Rail Europe (raileurope.com) – Finding all the rail schedules for traveling in Europe can be daunting, but this site helps you find the schedule and train that fit your itinerary. Also, remember to check out the special deals section just before you commit to booking your passes since you might be missing out on some extra deals.

TripAdvisor (tripadvisor.com) – One of the original review sites online, TripAdvisor is still one of the best. Look up hotels, flights and restaurants while accessing tons of reviews on everything. TripAdvisor even includes free travel guides and trip ideas.

WebFlyer (webflyer.com) – This site is a great resource if you want to figure out the best way to maximize the frequent flyer mileages you currently have. WebFlyer will not only tell you how to transfer points between different airlines, it will also tell you how to stretch your miles.

VIII. One Last Note

This not only applies to budget travel but all frugal living advice in general.

Like you, I have read many books that promised to save me money. The books usually offer advice like "Do this and you will save." Some of them may be written by someone you know, while others are from an authoritative source that you trust. Some make so much sense that you feel dumb not giving their advice a try, and others are so persuasive that you might even dream about all of the possibilities they spell out after you finish reading.

So far so good, but what happens after a week? Half of the time, we forget about the tips altogether, and the other half, we assume the advice don't work when there are no results the next day. Other times, we tell ourselves that we don't have enough time to try out the advice and make it work.

Don't worry if this is you. Everyone is like this. We are busy and don't usually spend time debriefing after reading useful money-saving tips. After all, many of us read these books because we want to kill time or take a break from work, not to actually save a ton of money. Disagree? If you read this book because you wanted to save big, shouldn't you be taking notes (especially since I already asked you to do so)? If you really want to save big, why didn't you? If there is one piece of advice in this book that's the most important, it is this – **Take Action!**

Perhaps this is the writers' fault (myself included) because we do not always mention the dedication it takes to save big. I'm sure many of you already know many of the tips written in this book, but in order to truly save, hard work is involved.

We make excuses for ourselves and complain all the time about why everything is so expensive. We complain about authors not giving enough detail, we complain about our circumstances and we complain about why it works for others but not for us. What we really are complaining about is why no one does all of the work for us and just gives us money. Whoever said frugal living is about doing nothing? Saving money requires time and effort. Wake up.

Don't have time? Stop procrastinating and make time! Go to that extra travel discount site to check on deals. Study the currency rates to make sure you are taking the smartest route; call the hotel to see if you can get a discount even though the website said you couldn't. The biggest mistake is to wait and not do anything. Don't be a casualty of inaction. Don't let life pass you by without saving big on your travels because "you did not have time."

Make time. Reread this book. Practice the tips and save big.

It's Not Hard.

It Just Takes Time.

You Can Do It.

IX. Notes Section

Write down all the ideas that you come up with here to help you remember to apply the tips next time you travel.

No action. No savings.

Notes Section Continued

Notes Section Continued

The Little Budget Travel Book

Notes Section Continued

The Little Budget Travel Book

Notes Section Continued

Special Bonus - Frugal Newsletter at MoneyNing.com

Want to learn how to **invest wisely, live frugally**, and **stay debt free** but most importantly, **BE HAPPY** for free?

Go to MoneyNing.com/Budget-Travel-Book/ and type in NEWSLETTER to learn more. Many have done it and love the free content!

Here's what you will get:

- 7-Part Mini Course for a Simpler, More Frugal and Happier Life.
- More Money Saving Tips Delivered Regularly
- Newsletter Exclusive Offers Not Available Anywhere Else
- All For Free

About the Author

David Ning grew up thinking that saving money was the number one priority, but daily interactions through the years taught him that there is much more to life than just trying to retain every penny.

As he progressed through his life and learned more about the real meaning of frugal living, he started to understand how to maintain a unique balance for an enjoyable life that now helps him sustain a healthy relationship with his family as well as remain true to his core frugal nature.

David Ning now runs a personal finance website at **MoneyNing.com** where he helps millions of readers save money, be happy and achieve financial wealth by teaching, sharing and motivating everyone to better oneself.

Printed in the United States
152257LV00001B/160/P

9 780984 123704